I AM: You Power This Life
∞

By

Sia Alexander Brume

Seek ye first the kingdom of God and all these things
will be added unto you.
-Matthew 6:33

Dedication

∞

To You

Chapters

∞

I AM: You Power This Life

∞

Foreword

Everything that occurs from this point on reinforces your journey into Light. "Be still, then, and know that I am God." Psalm 46:10. Every situation and circumstance is caused by you. There is nothing outside of your dominion. Having constant attention and intention with regards to a thing will manifest that thing. It will be presented to your awareness, fueled by your own thought, momentum and direction. Below the surface of daily appearances is a massive current of energetic light which functions as a motor to drive your thoughts and feelings into actuality. This energy or light power is Divine, inexhaustible and indestructible and will be made manifest, without fail, into whatever conscious function you channel it. Think of yourself needing money, for instance. Automatically, this starts the flow of substance in and through your material being. As you begin to dwell upon the apparent limitation and lack of it, however, the flow gets dammed. You literally turn off the light by limited thinking. God is the substance behind this Light and as you come in tune with this Holy Presence, the true Power of your life is ignited. Let us begin to enlighten, now.

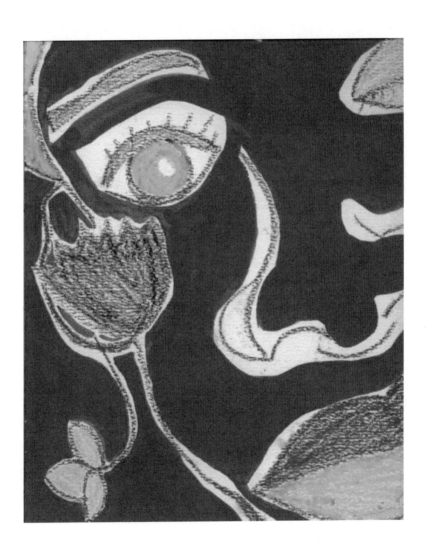

Chapter One

The Self

There is a Self in you that is in all things. It is a supreme Self, Divine and eternal. It does not die, become ill or experience lack. It never falters nor fails. This Self is who you really are and awaits only your recognition for it to fully blossom and shine forth in and through your life. This Self is an expression of the great and bountiful Self which is God. And as God is Spirit, so this Self expressed as you is also Spirit. There is absolutely no separation in this Self. It is in unity with the One-All-Self, the Spirit of God. Take time now to identify with this Self whom you really are, that which connects you to all things in existence.

If you fear success, know that your fear has no real power. You have already succeeded into eternity. Your achievement is absolute. Let go of the seeming fear and embrace joy. Turn your heart and mind to the glorious existence before you. What perfection is at hand! Look at this lovely spiritual creation, so enduring. Gratitude is the only answer to the overflowing bounty that is pouring forth through you. You cannot stop this wellspring. Let it rush forth; let it flow copiously into your being, expressing the unique radiance of your particular vibratory frequency. Oh, my, what a glorious beauty to behold!

Now

Be always calm, even when your emotions seem to flare. Relax into the awareness of the present moment. In stillness, approach each occurrence, keeping attuned to the everlasting current of unity and love running through each moment. This current will lead you indefinitely to an infinite possibility of perfect people, situations, experiences, opportunities, insights and discoveries. You become a magnet for wonder and Grace, such that the Spirit of Love is constantly glorified

3

through you and your life. Let it happen now in the stillness of your being. Walk consciously into the dimension of Love where all things are in perfect harmony - in harmony with the all that is, the Almighty, Most-High Creator. Do it now. Yes. How wonderful it is. Embrace what you want to create and watch it come to life, without delay. Ask for that which you require and witness the very realization of it right now. Speak your vision and be met with its perfect expression here and now. Call forth the appearance you choose and look forward to the easy and effortless restructuring of circumstances to math your vision. Know the Truth and see the Truth free you from all lack and limitation.

You

Every aspect of your life is a result of your inner state of mind. There is nothing outside of you that is responsible for each and every experience you encounter. If you choose a certain direction with your

4

thoughts and beliefs, the like condition or experience will follow. Make sure to align all thoughts with your true vision and be firm in your commitment to positive, constructive thinking. Do not allow the idea that circumstances beyond your control can influence or affect the outcomes in your life. Choose always to enter into a union with Divine consciousness. You in communion with God alone have the power to affect every outcome. There is only one Cause, that of Spirit and that Cause lives in you and you in It. The degree to which you acknowledge and express the Spirit of God within your temple body is solely responsible for the quality of your life. Nothing else! It is in your hands to channel this Spirit according to your expectations. Accept this and move in the moment knowing that you determine how Truth reflects itself in your life experience. Your steadfast focus on the One power within as the absolute driver for every experience, is that which will create miracles.

All that you see examine it and ask, 'Why did I create this?' Without judging it as good or bad, right or wrong, ask, 'what thoughts might I have entertained that led to this?' Your environment mirrors your inner world. All your thoughts strung together create the outer appearances. Stop thinking that there is a power outside of your being. There is nothing outside with power over you. The omnipotent God is all here, right here in the silence of your own heart, the stillness of your own being. Nothing can keep you from the good that awaits you. You are magnetic to it. Your good must come to you. It has no other place to go. It is made for you, formed by your deepest visions and loftiest goals. It is to be fulfilled in every area of your life, every aspect. Once you fully understand and accept that there is nothing keeping your good from you, beyond your own false thinking, then it will come rushing toward you. You will notice good coming forth in every area once you decide to allow it, to let it flow forth. When you know that you alone can block its expression; that you are the only one

6

in the way; that the whole world will conspire in your favor the moment you turn wholeheartedly to your good and accept it as your Divine birthright, then it will flow ever forth. Allow it now! Don't delay. Your good has been dammed up long enough.

Money, for example, may trickle or stop completely its flow toward you, simply because you believe the source of it to be outside yourself. You may see this source as very judgmental and assume you don't deserve the honor, the attention, the overflow, the love. Yes, can you fathom that? The source of money loves you. God has unlimited resources ready and eternally waiting to flow to you. Will you allow it? Can you let it? Yes, is the answer. So be it. It is done then. Accept your inheritance. Receive your wealth. As the current of monetary currency is making its way toward you, 'act now as if possessing all things.'

Does your health seem compromised? Do you have disease symptoms, so called chronic ailments? Who has given you these things? What is responsible?

Did your body turn against you by some power inherent in it which you do not control? Is the weather, genetics or some contagion to blame? Of course not! Because none of these seeming causes has any real power outside of your mind. You have given the source of your health a mistaken identity. The source of your perfect health is a loving Being. A Being who gives to you fully and freely a wholeness beyond compare. Say to your body temple, 'you are perfectly whole now, at the command of Spirit.' Watch as your strength, beauty and youthful brightness shine forth like gems.

And what of your relationships? Do they always fail? Or are you suffering from resentment, animosity, rejection and hostility with your mate? Ah, the illusion of separation. There seems to be a mate with whom you disagree or no fitting mate at all. But in truth, there is none other but yourself; you projected onto the body of another. The challenge begins within. Whatever unresolved inner self judgments, negative expectations, guilty associations you have will show forth in your

8

partner(s). Your false thinking will be expressed in the form of those you attract. As you begin to love freely that which you are in essence and to see in others this same essence, worthy of being loved unconditionally, you will have mastered the most important relationship you can have - the relationship with your Divine Self. As a result, others will be drawn to the you who is whole, happy and at peace. Then your relationships will become a benediction, an enlightenment, a joy. Your real Self is the Self of God. Love It first and foremost, with all your heart.

Grace

No more time will be wasted on the dwelling in lack, failure or problem. Knowing now that there is no external cause for these maladies, you will cease to give them your power, will and attention through worry, fear and doubt. If you have an appearance that you don't like, starve it of energy by placing your attention on that which you do like and then allowing your good to come to you. Or more accurately, flow from you. Your good is ever present, right here, right now. Claim it and embrace it. Happily recognize the wondrous presence of all the good around you, in and through you. See it, now! Time cannot distance your good from you. It is at hand. It is the quality of your Divinely inspired mind. Realize it. Look unto it. And above all give thanks, for your good is come!

The essential truth is that you have the power within you to shape the appearances in your life. You have a control given to you by God. If you want to bring something into manifestation, then acknowledge first that you have it within you already! This is the bottom line, the essential truth. You form your reality moment to moment, day by day with your thoughts. Your reality is shaped by what you envision and will always be a reflection of it.. As your envisioning faculty is directly linked to the creative Spirit within, and that creative Spirit is God, you must make use of this faculty for good. It is not the images that you see or that which you sense with your physical senses which represent what is real, but the state of your mind and your being in the present, all-powerful, wise moment. And in this moment you will find God. This awareness of the now being all there is, is sufficient to energize any probable material reality into existence.

Allow Grace to create your life experience. Cease to dwell in a mental/emotional space of doubt, fear and worry. Immediately upon noticing these characteristics in a thought or a feeling, change the direction of your attention. Know that you are using powerful energy and this energy will express in whichever direction you focus it. Know that no outside force is at work here, no future beyond your control and no past with power to further influence. Center your awareness in the Truth of the all-powerful, present moment. Realize that God is all here, right now and you have the opportunity to choose whichever probable reality that you envision. Each thought connects with the next one into a chain of

11

creative links. Choose definitely positive thoughts. Upon the approach of false thinking, stop and allow the full magnitude of the Truth of the one Creator within you to elevate you. Like a light that is turned on in a dark room, let the realization, your recognition of the luminous power of your ever-present Divinity, quench the onslaught of thoughts of despair, lack and confusion.

These negative thoughts evolve from a belief in a power outside of your Divine Self. This belief is false. There is no other power but God. Nothing can hurt you, halt you, impair you, threaten you, fail you, limit you or in any way affect you – a fully integrated and whole being. You are under Grace. This is your true state of being and there is literally nothing else that need occupy your attention but this simple yet profound fact. Forgive yourself constantly. Stop judging, blaming and criticizing, both within yourself and of others. Forgive, Forgive, Forgive. Let go and surrender all judgments, good and bad, right and wrong, rich or poor. Let them all go! Accept the Now as it is. Look beyond appearances and see the glorious Light shining forth from every expression. See God everywhere. Be a witness to the power of Light in your midst. Reflect the Light. Dwell in it. Be still in the Light. Inhale its essence. The more attention you give to it, the brighter it will shine. It is your own luminous Self, the radiant essence of your being - God's perfect seed in you and in all things. Water this Divine seed with your conscious awareness, through gratitude and faith. And watch as you grow from Grace to Grace until all that exists for you is the purity of who you are – love, joy, peace, contentment, success, prosperity and wonder. Let not yourself be distracted by the false presentations of an illusory world. Stay in the realm of Truth and you will be blessed by the anointing of the fountain of living Light, the sun of God, the I AM powerful in the presence of the Light. You can create anything you desire, live whichever life you choose, now. Accept this Truth and move forward into the Light.

15

Chapter Two

The God in You

I see that you are ready now to accomplish, to achieve, to succeed, to prosper. Good. For now is the appointed time. Today is the day of the added things. Yes, you are chosen to receive. You have chosen to receive. Open your eyes. Open your hands. Open your heart. Clear your mind with the soft stream of illuminated light which is now flowing in and through your consciousness. Know yourself as one with that prayer which you have offered forth. See the free-way, the path strewn with roses. It is done. Your dreams are realized. You have made the claim. The fruit is ripened. Take and eat. Eat of the body of Spirit, the everlasting sustenance. You may think that food can harm you or heal you. This is false thinking. Nothing external has any power over you. For the external is illusion, dream, a mirage. Bless it, yes. But do not give it power. You are the power. Let the food be blessed by you as an expression of the energy of perfect Spirit. It is Spirit reflected in apparent form - free, pure, loving Spirit; full of creative, productive, prospering power, endowed by the Spirit of God, alone. Let your mind know this and cease to think falsely about anything ingested. "It is not what goeth into a man's mouth that defiles him, but what cometh out."[1] Be at peace with the food you eat. Know it as Spirit, only. Surrender to the perfect flow of Spirit in and through you - wonderful being, sweet truth in action, joyful presence, loving kindness expressed. One fearless doer empowered in all-things, speak now of your great understanding, your perfect peace. Reveal your shining light before every apparent thing. Be who you are, now. I call you forth. Come, now! Make a joyful expression unto this life. Gather it all together and show your wholeness. As you are recognized in all your fullness, let all seeming, all else fall away. With deep

---

[1] Matthew 15:11

17

gratitude and praise, I call you in the divine salutation; I speak your name - Holy. And firmly standing in stillness, I wait knowing you are here and "It is done!"[2] The time is now. Give thanks. Rejoice.

The Law of Love

Live by the law of Love. Bless everyone that you see, for they are the face of God come before you. Praise everything that you hear, for it is the voice of God come to speak to you. Find joy in all that you do, for it is the activity of God moving through you. Be at peace with all that you are, for you are the expression of God being perfected in you. Show kindness to all whom you meet, for they are the body of God come to greet you. Rejoice in every situation that confronts you, for this is the plan of God at work within you. Love each and every moment given you, for this is the grace of God living as you,

---

[2] Revelations 21:16

being glorified through your every breath and inspiration. Once you open your mind to receive the boundless glory of God's perfection, opportunities will spring forth out of the woodworks, so to speak. Do not become overwhelmed or even too distracted or emotionally involved with those appearances. They are but reflections of your consciousness' burgeoning understanding of its power and true place within the infinitely creative universal matrix. Know that energy is moving toward you in wonderful, unforeseen ways to bring you closer to your good and your good closer to you, in manifest form that is. No need to worry or fear, these conditions will work themselves out. You do not need to revert back to struggle, doubt, and anxiety. Simply accept that your good is manifesting perfectly and its form is in the process of becoming, just as your divinity specifies.

After a time of seeming aloneness, scarcity and boredom, a great influx of creative opportunities, people, circumstances and substance will pour forth from you.

You will be inundated with offers, gifts, proposals and the like. Do not try and figure them out in a mental, strategic way. Let them flow with the Spirit of love, from whence they came. Spirit is omnipotent, remember this. It does not necessitate your human thought in order to gather itself together into perfect form. Be still and know that God is at hand; that the perfect outcome is imminent. And meanwhile, give thanks for the plethora of good things in your midst. You are a divine magnet and so long as you stay centered in this truth, your good cannot resist you. Take your mental effort out of your affairs for a time. Let your fears dwindle through attention only on, "the peace that passeth all understanding."[3] Do not try to figure things out. Accept them. Be thankful and let it be! Your help is not needed, save a firm stand by the principle of the living God at work in and through every facet of your life right now.

You may be shocked at the wondrous opportunities that abound for you at this time. Resist the

---

[3] Phillipians 4:7

urge to sort them out, talk about them or even contemplate them. Stay in the realm of Truth. You are the creator, the master, the one and only real power and presence in all this you see through your oneness with the most-high God. This truth is your heritage in Spirit, the one God who made you, liveth in you, the holy temple. "You are the temple of the living God."[4] Let go and let God, then. There will soon come a moment when all the good flying everywhere about you will settle in on itself in a very perfect, exact and timely way. You will surprisingly find yourself in a situation so ideal, it will seem as if a dream. All your requests will be answered. Every vision fulfilled. And you will be suspended in an embrace of pure Light so sustaining and invigorating that all will be at ease with you. Every good thing will surely come easily for you now, as you are walking in a state of Grace. This Grace has become the true meaning for you and your life. All else is the reflection of this

---

[4] 2 Corinthians 6:16

21

great blessing, this benediction, this anointing of Spirit upon you and all that you see.

You are free now to enjoy all the wonders of the bountiful Spirit of love at work in you. Continually be aware that every opportunity is a gift of God. Pay little attention to the form they come in, the people who offer them or the material benefits of each. Look only unto God. See Spirit made manifest. Praise God and commune with God. Talk to Spirit about the light that is meant for you to abide in through these opportunities. Ask for guidance in seeking this light. Abide in it. Give thanks. Be joyful. Expect the best and know that the Spirit of love, all-powerful and full of Grace does all things perfectly and without fail; and that these things, too, are God in action. Let the supreme action of the Most-High take charge in you and release all other false thoughts, emotions, beliefs or expectations. See God alone.

Balance

You may be offered an amazing position that seems perfect for you after a long period of no such opportunities. You may then be offered a wonderful endeavor that seems to conflict with the first. You may begin to feel confused and prepare to use mental and emotional strategies to resolve the dilemma. Stop! Know that your new state of mind is being challenged and tested in order to be reflected as outer harmony and balance in your affairs. Let the situations alone. They will formulate into a natural, balanced conclusion. Meanwhile, look for the light in each opportunity that comes your way. Begin to integrate these luminous rays on an essential level into your being. Let the vibratory frequency of each find its perfect radiance in Spirit. Do not get in the way of this balancing, by anxiously wanting an answer, obsessively attempting to force an outcome or enlisting the support of others to make a decision on what to do. Do none of these things. Simply

23

wait. Wait in the assurance that only good shall come from this. A beautiful restructuring is at work and all will reflect this beauty at the perfect moment. Take any lower vibratory energy out of the situation.. Set yourself on High in Christ consciousness – the, I AM powerful when anointed with the Light. These outward appearances are meaningless. The true value and prize is in the deeper re-leveling of your inner life to maintain a higher spiritual vibration, cleansed of past emotions, old fears and chronic negative thinking that have served you naught.

You who claim to have faith in God, in what do you place your faith? Your attention, belief, awareness, trust, conviction, commitment and acceptance are directed where? Is it in God as the one and only authority in your life, the Spirit of love as the one and only presence, the Divine principle as the only power at work in and through you? Or is it in something else? Is it in your job, career, relationship, bank account or body? Could you be worshiping social standards, material desires, philosophical doctrines, past experiences or future goals? Then, stop! Faith is the absolute worship of God to the exclusion of all else – absolute, unwavering, implicit faith. A covenant.

"Judge not by appearances, but judge the righteous judgment."[5] God is all there is. All seeming else is of naught. Be in a covenant with God. Truly, you are all-powerful as the mighty I AM presence within you, the spirit of the living God. Accept nothing less, for this is the absolute truth of your being. Doubt no more. Put your faith in divinity to work, consciously. See nothing but God. Look into the shining countenance of God in everything and everyone. Hear the voice of God. Listen. Be present in the here and now. Pay no attention to the clamor of the world. Let all worldly concern go. God is in complete control. Trust in the supernal, supreme grace of God. Give your life over to this one power, this force of Love. Let nothing else distract you.

---

[5] John 7:24

Nothing. The essential meaning is in God, the I AM that you are. Go within to this essence and stay.

Chapter Three

The Spiritual Path

That which is happening right now is purely spiritual. All the ineffective, outdated and useless thoughts, feelings and beliefs are being expelled through a material enactment of their misguided propositions. Spirit is shining a light on these misunderstandings and they are being cleansed from your consciousness through your mind, body and affairs. Stay tuned into your consciousness as you shift from the false to the real. Abide in your understanding of Truth and this will free you from all discordant manifestations - the false beliefs on their way out of your experience. Most of all do not be shaken by the forms before you. The Spirit of divine love is always the only force, the true power. And as you begin to recognize its dominion, you will witness its miraculous flow through every facet of your life. Be attentive, not to form or appearance but to the spirit of God at work in and through you.

Do not give up on your covenant with Spirit, no matter how daunting the appearances seem. Know that in an instant the omnipotence of the Most-High can be revealed in all its splendor, completely dissolving the false picture - especially when it comes to apparent financial distress and material obstacles. Firmly turn away from this illusion and praise the abundance of God that is really at hand. Be thankful that these beliefs in scarcity are exiting your consciousness. Bless the appearance of lack away and move forward into your new found recognition of Christ as a living light in your life, supplying you infinitely, abundantly, effortlessly without fail. Look unto Christ, the light, love and substance therein, with the full knowledge that it is the truth, the reality of your very being. When Jesus was presented with seemingly daunting and disturbing pictures of limitation, he praised the light of God that was at the root of these appearances. Instantly, the illusion or disharmony dissolved. Truth came to light and not a moment was wasted on anxious thought, feeling or belief. Across the board, Jesus knew that God is the all in all. With every faulty presentation, he did not need to reconsider or further question this truth. He consistently stood firm in the recognition of God - only. This unwavering faith led to a complete liberation from all discord and to an effortless unveiling of the miraculous truth behind all appearances. You, too, must have the mind of Christ. Rejoice at every turn in your mind, body and affairs. For every turn holds the seed of pure Truth and with your right attention will blossom into the rose of perfection - the activity of God.

Christ Mind

It must be realized that there is no halfway in this Christ-mindedness. There must be a complete recognition of Christ as the only true reality of every occurrence. Time must not be used to contemplate ought else. One must attune all awareness beyond appearances to the realm of light Divine, a dimension untouched by the seeming distortions of worldly illusions. Look beyond. See with the vision of Christ. Know that God alone is being made evident through every facet of your life experience. Be diligent and stay intently focused on the pure light of Christ shining about you and all that you see. Do not lose sight of this light for even a moment as the Truth awaits your recognition at every turn.

The key here is living with/in a joyful state of expectation and praise. This state is silent, calm and peaceful. It is kind, generous and innocent. A glowing, jubilant and radiant expression, this vibrant state is magnetic. Practice now the whole-hearted blessing of that which is before you as a perfect manifestation of the glory of God. Regardless of the appearance, know the actual to be God, the Divine love that is all that is. Literally, let yourself be in Joy at every moment's juncture with space and time. Praise, praise, praise without ceasing. Allow no other thoughts to linger, save the holy thought of Love's dominion. Yes, Love reigns, for it alone exists. As the divine state of being that is the Christ-mind, Love knows nothing but itself, all-powerful, ever-present and absolutely good.

Manifestation

In desiring a thing, you are declaring its close proximity to you. The idea of it sends waves of energy through living substance and starts the process of formation and manifestation. Doubting the possibility of the manifestation, questioning its probability or having anxiety about its timing will neutralize the activity of its substantial formation and unfolding. Waves of energy from thought are for the utilization and direction of spiritual substance into form. Confused thought equals confused manifestation. Be always constant in your attention to Spirit, Love and God, never wavering to consider a being, a process or an activity outside of

God's dominion. For remember, there is naught else but God; the pure Spirit of Divine Love which when fully recognized, never fails.

Do not take a passive approach, however, to seemingly inharmonious or negative conditions. Saying, "Oh, I guess it wasn't meant to be," or "everything happens for a reason." No. Stand firm and instead declare, "I praise this as God's perfection. All is well with me and I give thanks that only good shall come from this." We have been given the edict, that when times seem troubling, "Be still and know that I am God."[6] So, be still and know that I am God. Be still and know that I am God. Be still and know that I am God. Be still and know that I am God. Be still and know that I am God. Be still and know that I am God. Be still and know that I am God. Be still and know that I am God. Be still and know that I am God. Be still and know that I am God. Be still and know that I am God. Be still and know that I am God.

---

[6] Psalm 46:10

Be still and know that I am God. Be still and know that I am God. Be still and know that I am God.

With regards to manifestation, the Christ of God instructs us to, "Seek ye first the kingdom of God and his righteousness and all these things will be added unto you."[7] Let us unlock the secrets of this verse.

SEEK YE: Of your own volition you must look for the face of God wholeheartedly. No more asking for signs of that your desires, wants and wishes coming true. Not any longer gaping at others for their reactions, judgments and approval. Put an end to watching for external validity of your wealth and power.

SEEK YE FIRST: Primarily, above all else, you must look for the Light of God. Upon rising and throughout the day, before retiring and through the night, let every inclination be toward the Most-High. Let not a moment be spent on any musing but the I Am is God.

---

[7] Matthew 6:13

SEEK YE FIRST THE KINGDOM: Your inheritance is the fullness of God's divine majesty. Go after the riches of God. Find the almighty grace and glory in every moment. Venture into the holy temple of the living God which lies within the sacred place of your own being. Abide here. Where else shalt thou go? Might you seek out the temporal, corporeal or material kingdoms, glories and graces first and then vainly turn to God when all else fails? No. Your first attention must be to God, the only, the Holy Spirit of Divine Love. And here your attention must stay; standing firm, wavering not and with your entire being, single-mindedly seeking the dwelling place of the Most-High.

SEEK YE FIRST THE KINGDOM OF GOD: Have no other aspirations, allegiances or quests, save the realization of the living dwelling of the almighty God. This is the supreme good place, space and time that, in its perfection, exists effortlessly beyond these worldly limitations. The absolute good place within you, the Light of lights, the Love of loves is the dwelling place of God.

SEEK YE FIRST THE KINGDOM OF GOD AND HIS RIGHTEOUSNESS: Divine judgment is not the assessment made by human thought. You must allow the Spirit of Love to direct your attention to that which is true and real and not that which your senses suggest. God sees all things through the lens of the principle of supreme good. This principle is faultless and judges not by appearances. You, too, must accept the Divine viewpoint as the only angle from which you see.

SEEK YE FIRST THE KINGDOM OF GOD AND HIS RIGHTEOUSNESS AND ALL THESE THINGS WILL BE ADDED UNTO YOU: In recognizing the One as All, you achieve absolute dominion over everything.

37

Chapter Four

The Spirit of Truth

All the myriad scenes in your life's big illusion are aspects of you. There is absolutely no separation between you and it, them or that. All is one - the infinite expression of the One-All-Mind. Do not be fooled into believing the testimony of your senses. There is nothing outside of you. The Divine self within you, the living God is the actual substance of every appearance in your life. Honor it. Stop attending to the physical reality. Cease your preoccupation with it. It is not real. Like a dream, apparent reality has no existence beyond your consciousness of it. Now is the time to turn the light on. A sacred synergy is occurring between your understanding and the Spirit of Truth. The Spirit of Truth is not a philosophy, a doctrine or a belief system. It is a living, breathing, creative principle which resides in you - the temple of the living God. The Spirit of Truth operates practically and tangibly throughout all facets of your space/time self and energetically and vibrationally through all higher dimensions in which your Self may dwell. You must begin to live It. Let It live in you and through you without obstruction, mental or emotional. Every moment must be consecrated to the Spirit of Truth - God. Anything less is blasphemy.

Rise to the challenge of your Divine birthright and know the Divine principle as your absolute being. Be nothing else! This is essential. Now is the time to become devoted to the Principle. Though every condition may rise against you, stay in the realm of Truth and be not discouraged. A benediction is nigh. Fear not. "I am come that you might have life and have it more abundantly," and "I will never leave you nor forsake you."[8] This challenge apparent is but to prepare you for a cleansing. The clearing out of all that is not of you, the washing away of any trace of non-truth that may

---

[8] John 10:10

remain in the corners of your heart, mind and body. It all must go! Into the nothingness from which it came, it must vanish. As you let go of judgment, the flow of Love runs unobstructed through all facets of your being. This flow has powerful restructuring properties. It takes up all space and moves throughout time as infinite Divine love, causing a reshaping of your consciousness. You begin to know Love alone, as false beliefs are released through visible and tangible experiences. These issues and challenges are dissolving before your very eyes. Let them go, bid them a fond farewell. As you begin to live consciously in God at every moment, taking all thought away from the material, you will notice a clear shift in your relationship to the apparent world around you. First, you will become aware of a haziness, a fog around what was once clear, concrete reality. Things will appear nebulous and dream-like. Your feelings about the appearances will reflect this radical shift. You will find yourself floating a bit above the fray of it all. Situations and experiences will have little power over you, even though you are aware of their seeming importance and weight. A radiant pulsating energy of pure Light will surround you and fill your being such that you will no longer be preoccupied with temporal concerns. A natural working out and completion will begin to take place. All will flow easily and effortlessly for you, as if some unseen assistant is incorporating all of your best into a flowing expression. Opportunities will abound as your pure, light-filled energy opens magnetically to the field of infinite possibilities.

Being in Truth

You are now in full Divine expression and all your focus, attention and love in Christ is ready for fulfillment and manifestation. You are magnetic now. Good, wonderful and joyful experiences are at hand, being drawn to you, they are, by your own state of being. Accept and give thanks. Let the Spirit in you move freely in and through all manifestation, while you stay in a

41

place of peace and be still in God, knowing that all is well. Your body will begin to take on a higher vibration. All the functions will operate at maximum efficiency and grace. You will feel as if charged, invigorated by a force of such great love like you have not before felt. More sleep may be necessary, not due to exhaustion, but because you are being pulled to a greater understanding of your sensory experiences through dreams and a distancing from the material world. You may feel profoundly guided and directed, knowing things you wouldn't normally know and being able to do things you normally would not. You are now very aligned with Omnipotence. Therefore, you power is great. Due to this alignment, you will find yourself often in a state of pure presence. Your faith in the Spirit of Love is blossomed to a degree that you are ready to let situations alone, to trust in the great power of Divine Love, to manifest perfectly, without fail. In this way, your creative energy is in full force. Like the driver of a precision vehicle, every directional impetus is felt within the self and acted upon exactly. Be at your best, now. Know yourself as pure God energy and witness the perfect expression of this recognition, now. The light that you emanate is irresistible, it cannot be denied. It will attract a fullness of radiant, glorious, vibrant light particles set to take form according to your divinely inspired instruction.

At this moment in time it is essential that you stand firm in your covenant with Spirit. Remember, there is no other but God. Serve not false forms, ideas, or people. By "serve" is meant to consistently focus on, contemplate or otherwise attend to. Fear not for your future, but stand firm in the knowledge that all is securely in God's hands. Worry not about dilemmas and seeming obstacles, but stay true to your faith in the power of Love, almighty. Be present in the here and now, focusing on Truth alone. Truth represents the complete absence of a belief in lack, loss or limitation. It is a state of being one with the Almighty. Truth reconciles all questions, problems, or concerns you may seem to have. Dwelt upon, Truth resolves all seeming else. You are wholly free in Truth, right now. There is no condition which can withstand the flow of Truth in and through you. And therefore, no condition which can express anything less than perfection. Behave now as if Truth has set you free! There are no more obstacles in your path. Your way is clear, unhampered and joyous. Prosperity is your natural state and there is nothing at all to obstruct you, nothing standing in your way. Be cognizant of your supremacy in Spirit. Do not spend time complaining about an adverse situation, mourning a loss, or feeling sorry for yourself. Do not waste energy grieving a failure, pitying others or finding fault in any way. Your attention is a vital thing. Use it wisely.

Focus on the highest and the best. See the light of Spirit emanating through every form. No matter how discordant a situation appears to be, know the Truth about it. This is all you need do. Stay in the realm of Truth, always. Stay in the understanding that God is all there is, all present, powerful, wise and good. Know that your being at one with God's Truth sets you absolutely free. Do not accept negativity, disharmony, discord or limitation in any seeming form. Not even for a moment. Bless all and praise all knowing that all is the reflection of God's eternal perfection. Take no notice of the details of strife or struggle, pain or loss. Give thanks always for the perfect activity of God at work here and now making all things right. Feel the presence of the Spirit of Love as a real and vital force moving in and through you and all whom you meet. Find fault in no one and with nothing. Praise, give thanks and be in a constant state of forgiveness for every false claim that your senses would testify to you. Be firm in your stance with the Most-High. Have unshakeable faith in the perfect workings of the living God, eternally successful, prosperous and joyful. "Seek ye first the kingdom of God and his righteousness,"[9] and every seeming thing else will rise up in unity and grace to fulfill the glorious plan of the Almighty, the I AM, the All-That-Is. You are to be ready to receive the blessing when it comes. Your mind must

---

[9] Matthew 6:33

be open, free of all lesser thought, belief or attachment. An awareness of Truth must permeate every level of your being from your cells to your sight. Use your voice constructively and speak only when prompted by the spirit of Truth within. Do not use idle words to fill time and space. BE EXACT AND IN TRUTH with EVERY WORD, IDEA OR THOUGHT.

Divine Energy

Energy is God activity. Utilize it to create infinite expressions and manifestations of God. Let the Spirit of Truth inform all of your actions. Let yourself be a channel of Divine Love at each and every moment. You are not bound in any way. All perceived limitations are false perceptions, misguided interpretations of God's boundless Truth. Do not attend to limitations. They are not real. They do not exist, these false forms. In actuality, you are the perfect point through which God's infinite power emerges. Sharpen your focus and know

God alone. Be precise in your dealings with the world. For it is an illusion and has no power, save what you offer it with your thoughts. It cannot stand in the absence of your attention to it. Accept nothing the world offers as truth. Look to God alone. God alone exists and naught else, never anything or anyone else. Know this Truth and live it! With all your heart, mind, body and soul, praise God. Love God. Have unquestioning faith in God.

For a time, you may question your place in the world. Slowly, you come to realize that there can be no place for you in an illusion. Your true place is above and beyond it all. Beyond. Your purpose is not in becoming more a part of the world around you, but in integrating all that your senses perceive into the one awareness with God. This will serve to elevate your experience of the "world", to the kingdom of God. Your place in the kingdom is as a joint-heir to the throne of the Most-High. The Christ Being, the 'I AM powerful when anointed with Light', which is present in all things shall sit with you in your perfect place in Divine oneness, Love and, "the peace that passeth all human understanding."[10] So do not be concerned with fulfilling your purpose on earth. Know that your purpose is fulfilled in heaven and as you wholly recognize this success in Spirit, all will come perfectly to pass in form. Form, however, is not your priority. Leave it alone. It is merely a reflection of consciousness. Focus then on yourself as a spiritual being, living by God's law in a spiritual world.

In this world of Spirit, emotions have no power. Only in the deceptive world of earthly illusion do emotional states hold rank. Once you know that there is no power outside of the Divine, then external things no longer have influence over your being. You cease to be a victim of emotions that are seemingly caused by that which is outside of you and beyond your control. You are able to become transparent to the tides of emotions which you understand to be reactions to false beliefs.

---

10 Phillipians 4:7

Identify always with the Self that is beyond reactions, judgments and the feelings that follow them. Know this Self to be untouched by the stream of illusion that runs constantly through minds lost in the sea of false thinking. As you do this, you may find a host of latent, stuck emotional storms come to the surface. You may find your apparent present circumstances unbearable emotionally and feel the brewing of an intense discomfort. This merely suggests that now you are moving beyond emotional submission and coming to a place where your true Self lives fully in the moment, free and open to the creative Spirit running through it.

Light

This Spirit, moving boundlessly, discharges all psychic debris collected from continuous false thinking. This debris gets materialized on its departure and as a result of your lack of attention to it, disappears for good. While it appears, see it for what it is - nothing! Do not be swayed by it, though conditions may loom large and emotions seem to run deep. Your true Self is risen. Nothing can stop the ascent of your understanding. With assurance and great promise, know that light is dawning, beauty abounds and joy awaits your recognition. The most thorough cleansing of your heart, mind, body and affairs is occurring. "Stand still upon your watch and wait, here cometh the salvation of the Lord."[11]

You will witness to the coming of a glory-filled life, where all is perfect, whole and complete. Every good thing Divine is done and at hand. Golden doors shall open before you and you will move in a circle of charm and grace untold. All your good, bound by years of false beliefs, will come like a waterfall rushing forth in you and through you. You will find yourself having more than enough, more than ever, succeeding effortlessly serving the Divine. Spirit shall show you the way, its Light and Love shall cover you and fill you, spilling over

---

[11] Exodus 14:13

into all that you do and everything that you see. You are anointed and in this place, you are powerful. The omnipotence of God is upon you and you cannot fail nor falter. All that you are brings forth good. You live in pure light. Your being is in perfect peace. With each breath, you create wonder and beauty; give forth power and grace. The absolute principle of limitless life is supremely at work in and through you. Begin now to praise the very ground you walk upon. All that you touch is Holy. Refrain from idle talk and be on your still watch. You are being called to serve; you are being guided and are at this time very strong in Spirit. Breathe in the high tone of Spirit. Inhale the dynamic vibration of Divine Love. It shall serve you as you serve it. Your service shall be by Light.

Practice now imparting Divine Light at all times to all that you come in contact with. Watch it transform. Praise the Light. Forgive all, continually, that seems to be in shadow. The shadow is merely a cry, a beseeching for more light. Recognize the Light omnipresent and call it forth. Say it aloud, think it, whisper it now and forever; "let there be light."[12] Every dark moment is a wonderful opportunity to make the call for more light. The call shall be answered every time without fail. Remember you cannot falter now. You are anointed by this very Light. The living Light has called you to serve. You are ready. You need not wait until appearances reflect the radiance at hand. Go forth now, visit unto the fourth dimension. Allow its profound presence and activity to be here and now recognized and accepted by you. You are the channel, the conduit, the vessel through which it shall pour such a blessing out upon humanity, that there will be no space to contain it.[13]

---

[12] Genesis 1:3
[13] Malachi 3:18

53

Chapter Five

The Still Voice

The voice of a Spirit guide may become audible to you now. You may sense a presence clearly. This is the activity of the Love of God come before you to insure that you want for nothing, that all is well with you and that you are loved. In the seeming external world many will express love to you, want to give to you, help you and support you. Many will reach out to you with opportunities and aid. Your presence for others may be alternately a beacon of light bringing them joy and elation and at other times an unnamed agitation causing them seeming discomfort and uneasiness, depending on their level of awareness. Let God's magnetic Love do its perfect activity in and through you. Accept and allow God to be made manifest in your life and, "judge not by appearances, but judge the righteous judgment."[14] The righteous judgment is the unconditional love of Spirit. The mind of Christ being the mind in you, know that Love alone is at work now. Your power is in your absolute and complete recognition of the God of love in every instance from now into eternity. You are doing this even now. Give thanks. Praise and forgive the seemingly contradictory thoughts, emotions, people, situations and conditions, for they are being spiritualized by the power of unconditional Divine love. You are not alone. You are in God; living, moving and having your being.[15] Let this be enough. Let this be all, for God is all. And, "thy grace is sufficient unto thee."[16] It is like a game, simple and fun. Look at every occurrence from moment to moment squarely and see it not. Your human senses have become spiritualized and you need perceive with them no longer. Those days are past. Every occurrence,

---

[14] John 7:24
[15] Acts 17:28
[16] 2 Corinthians 12:9

whether emotional, mental, physical, financial, material, relational, etc. is to be viewed through the lense of Spirit or Divine unconditional love. You are ready. Begin now. Saturate the energetic pattern vibrating with the frequency of illusion with the radiance of the Light of God.. Simple. Focus on Tight, Divine Truth, the pure substance of God and let it flow freely, wholly into whatever the moment holds. Then, watch the illusion fade and reality come to life.

Illusion

You need do nothing physical or external to bring this to past. Neither fasting, meditating nor praying is necessary; attending to the Light, alone, will bring about such a refining of your being that your vibration will surpass all forms and become an actual living light. Impervious to any seeming discord, others may begin to come to you for help. Those seemingly sick, poor or grieving will become apparent to you. Send them light and shortly, healthy, rich and happy ones will suddenly come into view. Send them light. Continue to focus on light and you will begin to notice not the trappings of human existence, the poles of good and bad. You will see the finer frequencies of Divine light and love moving eternally, infinitely through all, in all, as all. It is in this frequency alone, that you will find true meaning, commune with God and know Truth as a living principle. Let yourself spin with this current. Be in the One. Hold this frequency by tuning out the feedback of discordant thoughts. Bless others continually and forgive them their transgressed thinking. Loose them and let them go into the realm of Spirit to be transformed by Divine Light.

Any difficult situation or feeling that may seem to be caused by an external factor is actually a result of a belief out of sync with Truth, an unpaid debt, an attitude of annoyance, a child's fever. These all evidence a forgetfulness of Spirit and are quickly dissolved upon the recognition of the one and only presence and power, which is God. This recognition comes immediately as you saturate the appearance with light. Light of the Divine is within you, it is the substance from which you are made; it is infinite, inexhaustible and at-hand. You, simply, must call on it. It will surely come forth and revolutionize your world of appearances. For, this world is merely a reflection of the pool of your consciousness. See it aright and it shall be aright.

When you send light forth, it actually goes into the atmosphere and reconfigures the vibrational frequency, effectively altering the quality of the expression in form of the Divine substance in your midst. In other words form is upgraded by Spirit. Remember, you of yourself have not the power to alter anything; it is in your communion with the Light of God that dominion rises up within you. As the disciple John said, "I can of my own self do nothing, but the Christ that liveth in me, he doeth the works."[17] And what is being altered is not God's substance, but the way it is

---

[17] John 5:30

perceived by your consciousness on this level of experience and comprehension. It is really not necessary for you to dwell in any place less than God's perfection. This perfection is on hand for you, dynamic and certain, waiting for you to comprehend its activity. All around you is God's perfection in form, come to light before your light-filled gaze. Raise your vibration to the level of the Light. Elevate all thought to the sublime place of radiant perfection and luminous glory. Do not allow lesser notions to infiltrate the peace of your mind. Be resolute in your commitment to the Light. For the Divine Light of the supreme One is magnificent. All powerful, it is, and full of Grace. It cannot and does not know fail. There is no concept of darkness in Light, only the absolute purity of Itself. This innocence of purpose and activity is the fundamental substance of all success, prosperity and joy. All you need do is take hold of the ray of Light stretching out toward you and watch as it becomes your very own flame. Its radiance is encompassing your very being and emanating from every facet of you, from your very core. Look now at the highest thought that you can reach in your mind. Reach even higher and let all thought dissolve into the infinite wisdom of Spirit. See how the Light-On-High harmonizes the energetic pattern within you, transcending discordance instantaneously. Resting in the peace of God, know that there is none else here but you and God. The Christ mind is your avenue to the rich kingdom of God awaiting your recognition. As you feel this oneness, this unity, this communion, a Grace shall descend upon you and enlighten the whole of you, raising your being to a Divine dimension where you will clearly see and feel that there is none else but God. You will know that all seeming else never was and can never be your real life.

Life

You see now that your real life has always been and will always be, in God, in Love; never changing, always present, fruitfully blossoming and at hand. Please take a moment to realize the power in your Divine recognition. No-thing else can impact you, affect you or influence you. You are completely free of all worldly illusion. God is in your midst and that is all that is. Your power in God is infinite. Charmed is the life you live, so full of Grace that only God can touch you. You are now in the realm of Truth, supreme and overarching. The arc of Love has spread over your being and you rise now into the limitless Light of pure Divine power. With this power, do all. Speak the word and see it done perfectly and in Christ. Know now that all occurs in Spirit, first and only. With this knowledge, you may reach heights of expression so luminous and vital that all struggle subsides. There is no more conflict. Strife is ended. Know the Truth and be in it to the exclusion of all else. The Truth is freeing. It unequivocally sets illusion straight. It reveals the real, without ever entertaining the notion of falsehood. It is Truth, the righteousness of God. Once understood, Truth will raise you up to a place where you know that no seeming external thing has or could ever have even a modicum of power over you. You, in Christ, are all power. Your illumination in Spirit shall light your world, clearly and presently. Like Jesus, you can walk on water; you can heal instantaneously and hold the earth's elements in your grasp. You can look to any earthly mountain and say, "Be thou removed, be thou cast into the sea, and it shall do whatsoever you saith."[18] The miracle is accomplished by the power of Truth. "I am the way, the truth and the light," says Jesus the Christ.[19] Your vision of yourself as one with Christ and every good thing is the spark that enlightens the fire of consciousness in Spirit. Once lit, this luminous light shall flow as God, illuminating every apparently dark place. The Light shall dance across the field of infinite possibilities highlighting every good and perfect thing and bringing to the fore of your vision, the Divine vista - God's window. Any seemingly

---

18 Mark 11:23
19 John 14:6

inharmonious situation can be immediately made right through the turning of the attention wholly to the Truth Divine. Let not any claim - material, mental or physical – dwell in your consciousness. Abide in the actual Light, shining like the sun all around you, in you and through you. Reach within your being to the Most-High idea and stay there. Revel in the beauty of the celestial realm. How wonderful it is to be in the Grace of God, to reach the dimension of pure and perfect potential. Here, you make your reality. In this place your creative energy is powerfully vital and alive. You do shape every occurrence and experience from this place. In looking intently here, regardless of the external appearance, you rise up beyond the world of form and thought and dwell in, "the secret place of the most high.[20] This is the place of pure recognition - omniscience, omnipresence and omnipotence. "All power is given to me for supreme good in mind, body and affairs," here.[21] Nothing

---

[20] Psalm 91:1
[21] Matthew 28:18

external shall overpower you as you live in Christ, consciously. For you become the All-That-Is, the very substance by which the seeming external is made. You now determine the outcome, the result, the effect. You, as unified Spirit are the only cause, the one and only creative force. And therefore nothing can come to pass, save through your intent and purpose. Know this as Truth and accept it now. Be constant and abide always in the perfect joy-filled Light of Spirit. Celebrate pure Spirit, praise the Light and give all glory to God, the Most-High. Become the Light to all, for all and the Truth personified, forever and ever. Amen

Be prepared for a new life. For now that you are "in Christ, you shall be made new, the old things shall pass away and everything is made new."[22] Now is the time for newness of life. Be steadfast in your embracing of the Christ-mind. Without wavering, stay your mind on the Light of God. Give forth light with every breath and let your every word be a beacon of light, a vital call. You

---

[22] 2 Corinthians 5:17

shall rejoice now at the glory before you. "Ye are God's."[23] The face of God shall be your own and you shall dwell in a state of bliss eternal where the whole world shall become as one, unified in Spirit and in Love - the perfect expression of Christ consciousness.

Good

Whatever is happening now is Good. No part of it is wrong or troubled. It is in fact, Good. Perfect. Holy, even. Do you see the good before you? Is it not gleaming? Oh! Yes, how glorious it is, this present good. So full of the substance of God it is, the vibrancy of God made manifest. The living Principle personified. Your good is so real, overflowing and never-ending, it is. It alone, exists, without comparison or contradiction. Its influence and expanse is absolute. Your good extends deeply and widely, flowing through all paths you take. It is there now along this very path, so strong and flexible

---

23 Psalm 82:6

and glad. Your good is God – free, pure, perfect and eternal. It is your infinite Self being itself without limits, bounds or distractions. Move thought aside. "Let not yourself be troubled."[24] Do not judge your apparent situation. Be still. Feel the presence of the peace of God. Christ is at your side. Invite the Spirit of Love into the sanctuary of your heart. Stop trying and let go. Surrender your human persona to the sanctity of the one Self - God.

You have nothing to lose and can lose nothing. All that you truly have is a gift of God and can neither be taken nor given in a worldly sense. God's infinite wealth, wholeness and love is your birthright. It is yours by divine right. Embrace your bounty. In faith, ignore the clamor of the world's cries of scarcity. Remain untouched by falsity. Your truth is God's own perfection. Live in the serenity of this Truth recognized. Be not dismayed by the eruption in your personal, business or financial affairs. Praise through, be still and know the

---

[24] John 14:1

Truth. "And the truth shall set you free."[25] Your emotions may rear ugly heads; praise through. Your finances may hit rock bottom; praise through. Your work may falter; praise through. Your family may desert you; praise through. Your friends malign you; praise through. Praise through every appearance of the world of illusion, of every discord in your life until you become a witness to the Light of the Real. And then the picture is clarified. The veil is lifted. Dawn is come. As you praise through the apparent reality, the seeming strong hold of the external steadily falls away. The way, rules and laws of corporeal sense lose their false dominion. Seeming bounds about you dissolve and are revealed as the illusions that they really are.

While you once dwelled blindly in the false world of appearances and let illusion lay claim to your life, you now see clearly through God's window and are under no other law, but God's. It is a simple choice; yet a profound one. "Choose ye this day whom you will

---

25 John 8:32

serve."[26] If you choose to attend to illusions, they will grow big and loom large from the energy of your focus. You will feel at the mercy of circumstance, caught up in conditions beyond your control. Hopelessness and defeat may haunt the serenity of your spirit. Nothing will ever seem to go right, to work out. You may curse God or worse, resign yourself to a belief in no God. Though, the true choice is always at hand - the choice of Love. In Divine Love you are at once elevated above all worldly choice. You become decided perfection. And in this unity with the Divine, all else known to you reaches perfection and that is all there is. Silently, in stillness, acknowledge Love.

---

[26] Joshua 24:15

Chapter 6

The Divine Law

Go inside to the place where no human law can stand. The Law of Love alone shall prevail over you. This absolute Truth, and as you turn within to face its source, these living waters of perfection shall come pouring forth upon your life. The living waters of Truth, upon recognition, flow straight through earthly illusion, the dream of the world. In its flow, it carries away all claims of imperfection and discord and deposits this rubbish into the sea of transformation; washing you clean of false perception and belief, you who, "dwelleth in the secret place of the Most-High, shall abide under the shadow of the almighty."[27] The secret place is the stillness of your own being. It is the arena of the living

---

[27] Psalm 91:1

God in your midst, the Christ consciousness and mind of God in you. Be always in the Most-High place and God's perfection is then made alive in you.

God

There is something much greater than this apparent world, something far beyond the testimony of your senses, the good and the bad, the happy and the sad, success and failure, poverty and wealth. This ever turning wheel of matter and of mind is not real and solid, as it seems to be. Its rotations are mentally driven and are of no consequence outside of the limited awareness of the small human mind. This you see about you does not exist. It is, all of it, a projection of your mind. You, alone, define the characters, their play and the ending to the drama. The outcome of every situation in your life reflects your consciousness. Nothing is set, but God's Grace. All responds to you. Your identification with a victimized self, at the mercy of happenstance, gives power to illusion which can do naught else but what you instruct it to do, through your attention and awareness. Instruct your thoughts, ideas, feelings and emotions to be in God only. Instruct your experience to be a constant unfolding of God's glory. Nothing external to you has any power to affect you, because it does not exist. There is only one cause from which all else stems - one Law. This supernal cause is God. The Spirit of unbounded Love is alive in you eternally and every aspect of your life is under this Divine dominion. Turn your full attention toward this great Benefactor, this perfect power that produces only grace, glory and perfection. Once and for all, stop attending to a false reality. Tell your senses, "No." Let no situation, person or belief daunt your purpose in God. Stay in God, always. Do not accept the limited perception of the human mind. Look beyond to the greater Being, the true Self Divine, who is the Master of perfection, the Champion of glory and the King of grace.

Vision

Now begin to look up always. No matter the apparent eye-level condition, lift your eyes heavenward. Lift your heart and mind out of the depths of anxious thought and dull attention. Vision skyward, literally and figuratively. See God. The clouds shall speak to you then, as will the sun, moon and stars. The birds, even, shall share their song with you, their high-flying grace. Never be discouraged by the scene apparent from the downward view. Look not upon earthly experiences or situations for truth or validity. Keep your vision on the highest. Stay ever in the realm of glory, the dimension of Spirit. There is no truth to the claim of the senses. Things are not what they seem to be. God, alone, is present, at work and in view. With proper vision this reality cannot be missed - luminous, radiant, sparkling glory. Goals are not achieved through working toward some future ideal. Now is the only time. You cannot expect to accomplish a state of being within which you do not presently dwell. There is no you afar off that is wealthy, successful or full of courage. That spectacular you who lives in your dreams as the object of your strivings is present, right here and now. Its only home is the center of your present Self, in this very moment. All energy spent wishing, hoping and striving to become something that exists nowhere, but in the You at hand, is wasteful and unproductive.

There are qualities which you associate with the ideal you strive to be. It is these qualities which abound in and through your being at this moment. When recognized and accepted as readily available for your expression, they do come flowing forth with great power. And any mental, physical or emotional efforts that you can expend toward bringing forth your ideal only pale in comparison to the power of your realized oneness with God presently. You must understand fully that you are that ideal already and every urging for manifestation is simply your Being stating the fact of Itself. A misunderstanding of the true nature of your desires has occurred. You have mistaken longing for magnetism. The pull that you feel toward certain ideal manifestations within your life is never a passive wishfulness, it is a definite claim to the present reality of your victory in Spirit and in form. The voice of desire is actively saying, 'I am this very ideal now. Let my Truth be made manifest.' If you here it as, on the other hand, a cry of hope or as an anxious craving, you then begin to look outside of yourself to reach a goal that has no external origin. Consequently, you completely miss the mark and release energy uselessly in the wrong direction.

As a result, you may feel as if you are spinning your wheels and getting nowhere or that your achievements leave you feeling empty with none of the satisfaction you'd expected. Any object, position, person or place which you are compelled to seek outside of you is nothing but an expression of a quality or state of being which already exists within you – waiting to be acknowledged. Anything that you possess a deep desire to be or to have, you presently are, entirely and more. However, you will not see the evidence of this truth expressed tangibly until you are able to truly recognize it as a spiritual reality in which you presently dwell. When you at once realize that you hold, right now, within your hands the fertile seeds to the highest ideal that you can imagine yourself to be and you begin to "act as if possessing all things," then you will find every situation, experience, person and thing to be as sent by an Angel to make your every dream come true. And it will be a joyous coming forth of the highest You, your great Self who is here now awaiting recognition and has been all along.

Awareness

If you feel that you always seem to fail at achieving that which you sincerely want to accomplish, you are misguided by false thinking. You have only failed to see that within you is the present source of every good thing that you can ever imagine for yourself, your life and the world-at-large. You have succeeded at separating yourself from that which you have always believed to be outside of yourself and needful of being sought after. If you are honest in your heart with what you truly desire to be and to have, you will intuitively vibrate with this Truth. You will know deep within that the reality of your being is complete and absolute wholeness wanting for nothing in its infinite abundance. You will sense your God-given power to create and manifest easily and effortlessly that which is your present and eternal Truth. You naturally begin to tune into ways to align yourself with that Ultimate force and energy which is responsible for the existence of every substantial thing. This transformation is taking place now. You are undergoing a restructuring of beliefs that will be reflected in your experiences. Every occurrence now will be a symbol of your deepening awareness of your true place within the universe. There is a higher flow within which you have chosen to dwell. It is the

77

realm of Light, where substance, when called upon, immediately manifests into form. You find now that your thoughts are of a higher nature - light, clear and precise and that they are instantly reflected in your experience. You notice a shift in your perception, where you are largely unaffected by external happenings and remain consistently in a place of perfect peace. Yet, you are fully aware of the creative properties of your state of being and can see clearly how your inner reality is depicted across the myriad landscape of your outer life. The Light Divine is now clarifying aspects of your being that are out of alignment with Truth and quickly dissolves these misunderstandings. You begin to see the glowing presence about you and to feel Its comforting embrace. Your senses take on a higher function. You see the invisible and hear in silence.

The silence that you are experiencing where all is still and in dynamic poise is powerfully creative. You have planted a rich seed and are set to reap an abundant harvest of good. This is a time of gestation. Miraculous shifts are occurring which will bring about the creation of a new you, entirely. You are being born again. I can assure you that whatever you have asked for, yearned to be, will come to pass before you in ways that surpass your most lofty expectations. You will undoubtedly witness the perfected form of your long held inner desires. By dwelling in the kingdom of the Most- High, you charge your being with a power unmatched. Through your continued faith in the omnipotence of God, you have risen above the mundane laws of the human illusion and approached the sanctity of the Christ principle. And Christ has given his word that "whatsoever you ask in my name, believing, you shall receive it."[28] Be poised to receive. In stillness and in peace, let the Spirit of infinite Good come unto you. Watch as it its Holy presence envelopes you. Praise all as its Divine activity. Be a present observer, a witness of the flow of its power. Meet everything before you as God, Itself. God alone is in your midst. Be aware of the

---

[28] Matthew 21:22

perfect presence of the Divine round about you. Let it saturate your being. Allow the Light of God to be your singular focus. Steady your awareness upon the eternal presence of the high Spirit of Love, always abounding, ever fulfilling and ceaselessly offering itself unto you.

Presence

Into all that you do, place wholly your true Self, full of light and love. Give unto all as God giveth unto you. Let your every act be one of faith in the omnipresence of the Most-High. Do your work on behalf of Love, the eternal one Spirit. Offer your skill, creativity and intention upon the altar of Divinity. Do nothing half-heartedly or for any reason but for the glory of God. Aspire to ignite the Light in all you see, to bring forth the love of God, the Spirit of good, the one true Life, the eternal radiance of the Most-High. Go forward now with power and grace, standing firm within your true place in Spirit. Claim your oneness with perfect being and cast your light upon every seeming shadow of human thought, belief and experience. Be committed to a thorough alignment with Grace in all things. As opportunities arise within your human framework, utilize them to firmly stand in the heart of God's creation. Know yourself as mighty in Christ and become immersed in the light flooding your consciousness. Spread this Light with every cell of your being and welcome its illuminating presence into all that you are and everything that you do. Accept nothing, but the full bounty of God's perfect substance and activity. Let all else fall away and pay no attention to the false claims of the senses. For truly, there is nothing but God. No failure, no doubt, not worry, nor fear, no sickness, poverty, pain or loss, no limitation can remain in the presence of God. There is absolutely naught else anywhere in anything or anybody, but God, Itself. Know this. Trust this and exhibit unwavering faith, thereby.

Chapter 7

The Living God

If you have in any way feared the outcome of a situation, do not. You are the situation, everyone in it and its outcome. Within you is the living God, author of all that is. So you in Christ shall write the script. Do it now. Then, know fully that it shall come to pass by the grace and power of the living God. Rejoice, for your day is come. Speak the word and it shall be born of the flesh, now. Your creative power is unlimited and supremely good. Use it now, joyfully and with all the strength of God within you. "Lean not upon your own understanding."[29] (Proverbs 3:5). Put your whole faith in the wisdom of the omniscient One on High. Hear now the voice of God. This is the voice of love; the voice of joy, the voice of praise, the voice of encouragement, the kind voice, the generous voice, the voice of caring, the voice of sharing. Listen. You are being spoken to in Spirit, a benign generous Spirit who believes in you and deeply cares for your well being. The vibration of Spirit's tone is melodic and is inspiring you to reach the summit of your Self, the apex of your being.

---

[29] Proverbs 3:5-6

Loose all else that occupies your attention and focus solely on the call of Grace. Its delightful song shall resonate with your true Life within; and thus, you are uplifted beyond the throes of human existence into the realm of pure perfection and bliss. You are being guided through the infinite into the everlasting, filled with grace and saturated by love. You can hear it now. Listen. It only takes an instant for the sun to come from behind the clouds. Making big dreams come true necessitates a focus and determination not in the external realm, but on your inner consciousness and being. A steady attention to the state of consciousness within and its ascension in Light and Love will make a clear way for the realization of any goal. Your consciousness must match your intention and goal.

If your goal is to harvest roses, you must decide to grow them, preparing the soil, choosing the seed and aiming for the proper season to begin planting. You must then plant the seeds into the rich soil you have made, tending with steady, patient attention. Then, knowing roses are sure to come forth, let go and wait. Your consciousness is like the soil, align it with rich spiritual substance, the living God within. Once planted in the fertile soil of your consciousness and set by your positive intention, every good harvest shall come to fruition without fail. Allow it. Stand upon your watch and wait for the glory of Divine creative potential to be revealed in form.

Perfection

Keep in mind always that you are because God is. Say, 'I am because God is.' You are not because of your body, your mind or your affairs. Not because of your parents, your lover or your money. No form can make or break you, for it has not the power to create. God alone is the creative principle. Know your origin to be in God and that all created form is an extension of the activity of God. Be clear about your true place and while creating and manifesting on the earthly plane, honor Spirit wholly. Let shine forth God's wonder in all that you do, yet still recognize the illusory nature of all material form. Any attachment that is felt for form is simply a call for Spirit. This longing, desire, want for a thing symbolizes the cry of your true Self for Divine light. The illumination of Spirit enlivens your Self. Go deeper into the Light with each anxious clinging, grasping and yearning. Let there be Light upon all form and see God.

Despite the appearance of harm, destruction, loss, pain and death, be steadfast in your understanding that nothing real has been or could ever be touched by these seemingly potent powers. Remember, God is omnipotence. Your awareness of the One power is sufficient to release the old illusions' claim on your thought and belief. Thus, providing for you a glimpse into the eternal perfect moment where all is indestructible and safe. In your pure recognition of the now, you will find that nothing can hurt you, that you are perfectly supplied and that joy is at the ready. Flow into the sublime moment knowing that all seeming about you is fleeting, a dream. Put no stock in any apparent thing. It is but a mirage and does not exist within the perfect kingdom of Divine Love. In the perfect kingdom, the house of the Lord, all is supremely well. Look not at appearances that claim disturbance or discord, sorrow or pain. They are of the world of illusion, a dream world, vanished before the will of God. Nothing is wrong. All is well. Everything is Good, now. It cannot be otherwise. No matter what the appearance!

As you become more and more fluent in the language of Spirit, you will see the perfection all about you. It will be more noticeable than the false appearances ever were, until the appearances begin to fade altogether and you see only the face of God - the Divine visage. And like a dream, when you awaken, all identification with unreality fades away. Surely, you have recognized now the face of God in all your sensory experience. None of these things which you have grasped or clung to, have been real or true. God alone has been your desire and true longing; your savior and comfort. Not a person, place or thing can be credited with the key to your joy. No love has ever poured forth from man alone. The Spirit of the living God is in back of all that you see. Every good thing is come forth from the heart of God and it is to this One that you must turn now. Dropping all else and I mean all, turn and look unto the face of God. The countenance of the Most-High is shining in and through all that is in your midst. God alone has loved you, supplied you, secured you, held you, carried you and given you life. Let forms remain, but know their source as Divine. The eternal one is responsible for your every experience of good. Stop looking elsewhere. Stop looking outside hoping to find a job, a spouse, a dollar to satisfy you. Neither contentment, nor supply will come this way. Your true place of perfection is in God. All abundance is given unto you for your highest good in every area of your life. Yes, it is yours; receive it by recognition of the Christ mind as the one and only source of your infinite supply.

Begin now to cease your identification with appearances. They are not real, nor necessary or lasting in any capacity. God alone maketh real. God alone is true. Let go, now, of all false identification with the distorted messages of the senses and let God do and be its perfect Self. Appearances can reflect alone. There is no other power there. Be steadfast in your pursuit to "Judge not by appearances, but judge the righteous judgment."[30] Let not yourself be mesmerized by the claim of the senses. Be constant in your recognition of Spirit as the one and only true reality in all being. It is in Spirit alone that you dwell and in Spirit you are abundantly sustained, infinitely prospered and eternally loved. Abiding in Spirit is a continuous moment to moment pure recognition of the Truth at hand. This perfect Truth is simple, practical and powerful and to be trusted implicitly. God is All.

---

[30] John 7:24

Letting Go

Be not attached to form of any kind. Neither judge it nor condemn it. That which underlies every desired thing is the living God. God is the sole animating force of every good thing. And the spirit of the living God is infinite and eternal. It cannot be lost or stolen. It is eternally yours. Turn away from heart break, disappointment and despair. Turn instead to the bountiful face of God enlightened with eternal riches in love. Reach high with your vision and being to commune with the real source of your joy and the living waters will flow forever to warm your heart.

When I say look unto Spirit alone, I do not mean to pay lip service to this lofty idea. This directive is for literal use. None else exists but God. So, pay no attention to illusion. It is not your husband that is loving you, but God alone, through him. It is not your work that defines you, but the activity of God alone, through it. It is not your bank account which prospers you, but the substance of God only. Take forms lightly. Face God with your whole heart, mind and body until you drop all identification save with the Most-High. That thing you crave is not real, only the Spirit of God reaching in and through your life, is. Give thanks for the thing, but praise the God that makes this reflection of love possible. Know that your striving for career success is naught but God's aspiration of ineffable glory in and through you. Attend not to the details of your career, but to your partnership with God. Covenant with the Spirit daily, from moment to moment. Trust entirely in the One, to the exclusion of all else. Have full faith in God as the only one and worship no other person, place or thing. Be in God now. Rejoice in the fullness of the Christ mind. Be strong in God, the Spirit of the living waters and know this as your true source and power. Give no false glory to material powers. They are naught. Truly, God alone gives every good gift that shall come by you "heaped up, pressed down and spilling over."[31]

---

[31] Luke 6:38

(Luke 6:38). Where the thinking, reading and writing ends, you must begin your communion with the Light. "You are surrounded by the pure light of Christ into which nothing negative can penetrate and out of which only good shall come."[32]

---

[32] Ponder, P. 165

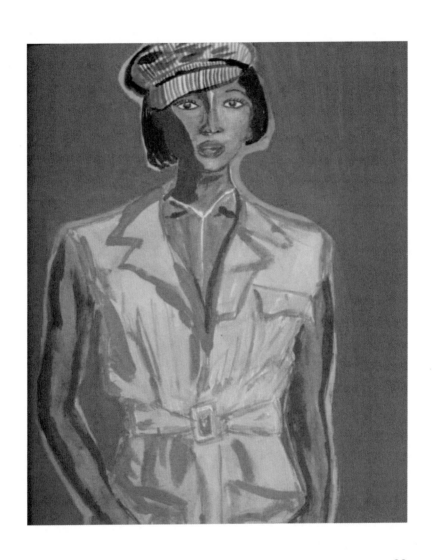

Chapter 8

The Peace of God

One of the most vital attitudes of mind to maintain is that of stillness and peace. Being of still mind is a life giving stream to your entire self, your consciousness. Contemplating the one Principle to the exclusion of all else elevates all that you are to your true state of glory in God. The fulfillment that comes from the single reflection on Eternal Being is unmatched. In this Divine serenity you are absolutely free, totally loved and infinitely supported. There is no higher place but the communion with God one finds in a still mind. Love is never in form. It, love, always resides in Spirit. Once you begin to look for love as a tangible thing, it is lost and attachment takes over. Spirit does not need to possess or contain. Spirit is voluminous and free. It is, within itself, sufficient. Spirit in love is boundless and forever ascending. When love is pocketed and held onto with an anxious projection on the beloved, it slips away - lost in preoccupation and wanting. Let love rule, in and of itself. There is no need to cling to it. Love is infinite. It is given unto you, freely. Simply allow it and fear not. It is coursing through your being even now. In fact, it is the life of you, your very breath. Make no special effort to contain it, look not upon any certain person to express it. Just let it be. Love is.

Love will always be thwarted in its expression by objectification. So, do not give love a name nor a face, save the eternal visage of God. You, as eternal being, are Love. Reach within with all your heart and find the spring of love that is inexhaustible - the pure devotion. Upon doing so, you will find that every encounter is in Love. Every friend on the road is a beloved. Every endeavor is a romantic interlude with Divine loving. Time, space and body are irrelevant. Love is constantly pouring forth into expression. It thrives in the midst of your pure recognition and revels in its endless dance. At a moment in time it may shine forth so brightly from the eyes of another, glow with radiant intensity from the touch of another. Yet, do not confuse this other with the eternal spring of illumined Love. Give thanks, yes. But, while steadily letting go of all attachment to the form of the thing and allowing the true Spirit of Love to abound in and through you touching all, without end. Love is a river flowing endlessly throughout myriad people, places and things that it encounters through you on your walk through illusion into supernal Light. Let it flow.

Being

There is absolutely no being apart from Divine Being. Nothing that seems to exist separate from God is real. There is no self, save God. Once this Truth is fully recognized, accepted and practiced all seeming loss, lack, limitation and discord shall fall away. Nothing but God can exist in the Light of God and the Light of God is all there is. Therefore, all that is around you, the furnishings, foodstuffs, friends, relatives, daily plans and

96

worries, physical ailments and social constructs are of naught, in and of themselves. God alone is the Self. At once, when you realize this fact, your life shall be changed. God alone is what you are and everything you see. All experience is God in motion, naught else. God is perfect, whole and complete and so is all that you can experience. Let the tide of understanding rush over you. Yes, it shall enrich all your affairs, enliven your body and enlighten your mind. Hear this. "There is no selfhood apart from God."[33] The Light of God is all around you, ever-present radiance. Stay in the present moment and without fail you will be a constant witness to the Divine illumination. All that is real is perceived in the Light of God. There are no limitations in the illumination you can receive by dwelling in Holy radiance. All Truth shall be shown unto you. Your faith shall be made substance. Nothing shall be impossible to you and you shall go from Light to Light and from Truth to Truth.

---

[33] Goldsmith, P. 88

There is never anything out there, external to you. To be affected by external situations, conditions or people, is to exist in a state of false identification. Turning within, one sees the Omnipresent power in all its wisdom and glory. From this point of power, we articulate our life experience. Through our thoughts, words and deeds, we channel Omnipotence into apparent form. In God, we find absolute perfect cause and as we tune into this living power within us, we cease to identify with externals and the external relinquishes to infinite Spirit. To free yourself from all limitations, you must recognize that you as true Self and worldly problems cannot exist, simultaneously. In whatever circumstance you seem to find yourself right now, the recognition of yourself as the living God in expression shall be an instant and eternal solution. If you know that God is omnipresent, how can you entertain the appearance of any discord, strife or struggle? Choose your God, this very moment and worship the Most-High, alone. "Choose ye this day."[34]

Gratitude

Quantity is irrelevant. What matters is the quality of your gratitude for that which you have before you, right at hand. Your appreciation for the bounty contained within the small symbol which you possess determines the extent to which the increase may flow in visible, tangible form. It cannot be stated enough, praise daily the substance at hand and you will by Divine law open the flood gates for the elemental nature sustaining this small symbol to pour forth into expression to meet your every single need. Lack is not a real phenomenon and has no spiritual foundation. In the universe, there is not a place where abundance fails to rule. Without the interference of human mind, all would eternally flow with unfaltering precision and perfection. Any substance when looked rightly upon is sufficient to call forth the supreme bounty of Spirit to unveil its wonder. There is never any point of lack in reality; only in the mind of

34 Joshua 24:15

man do we find the illusion of limitation taking hold. As soon as God is singularly envisioned within one's consciousness, God's bounty is recognized and experienced. And God is absolute abundance, total perfection and indomitable power. Look up now and see the wonder. It abounds and fails not.

You can in no way suffer, struggle or strain when you open up your consciousness to receive the prosperity of the Most-High. Praise the $1 as if it were the $1 million, for in both symbols you find the self-same substance - God, the I AM powerful in the presence of the Light. Never despair when you seem to have to little, not enough or less than you need. The appearance lies. There is no truth there. God alone is present. God's abundant substance is at hand, always fulfilling, forever at your beckon call. Can you look to the boundless sky and see the form of every desired thing? Let your imagination take flight and form in that infinite space which is God's countenance, alone. Envision Good only. All is so full to bursting with abundant rain, that which will water your driest dream, bring to harvest your richest bounty. Look up and see the fulfillment of every yearning for good, every call for greatness and humbly accept its present reality, the newness of its all-powerful presence. You stumble upon a penny, a pence, a cent, you pick it up and give thanks that the wealth of God is being made visible before you. Then give a smile, to each passerby, share your joy, for you have struck gold! You have come into your Divine inheritance, looked upon your true face, found the sacred in the ordinary - the Divine in you.

Chapter 9

The Real Life

At times the world outside will feel glaring with its apparent falsities and misconceptions covering all like a blanket of doom. You may be compelled to retreat from the constant illusion that is the world you see. "Be still," is the command. "Stand firm upon your watch." Remember that, "all the power has been given you for supreme good in mind, body and affairs."[35] In spite of all appearances, you are being elevated beyond the cares of the temporal world. You are being welcomed into the dimension of spiritual perfection. You are being cleansed by the fiery flame of Divine wisdom. You are being purified, enlightened and made whole. Let the wave of successive detachment release you. Allow the separation from the things of this world to take you fully

---

[35] Ponder, p. 30

through its surface turbulence into a place of Divine indifference. This is not apathy, so fear not. The dimension of Christ consciousness is a deeply felt state of absolute oneness with all creation as supreme perfect good. This recognition of Divine oneness brings with it a peace and contentment so perfect and sublime that the world will finally melt away with all its false cares, concerns and rules.

Transformation

Give yourself over to the transformative power of Spirit until you feel yourself flowing freely along the river of a doubtless, carefree, all sustaining embrace. On the other side of this profound immersion is an immeasurable peace with yourself and your real and true inner world, free from illusion. There is a Holy mountain which you must scale by going around and around its edges and inner routes. You may feel as if you are going in circles, repeating mistakes, never progressing, failing to move forward. You are not! The distance between where you are now and where you want to be can be covered by belief. That is the only real factor separating you and your Good. Your belief in the reality of your perfect good must flow through your emotions, thoughts, ideas and actions.

What are you feeling at any given moment? Are you content, joyful, at peace and optimistic? What are you thinking when your mental faculties are on automatic? Are your thoughts purposeful, kind, appreciative and constructive? What do you consistently remember about the past? Are you recollecting wondrous experiences, amazing accomplishments or loving encounters? And when you dwell on the future, do you expect the best, envision glorious opportunities and see things going from good to wonderful? When your belief is firmly rooted in the one God power, you think and feel in ways that exalt. You focus on and construct positive scenarios of both the past and the future. You become attuned only to that which is good, never wavering. And your life essence streams forth in joyful spectacular form. You literally become a magnet for all the wonder this universe has to offer. It is your attunement with Truth coursing through every part of your being as pure belief or faith that aligns you with all the good which you envision. Do not look upon a thing without blessing it. Let kindness spill forth from you despite the encounter. The surest way to secure your good fast is to bless everything and everyone continuously, to see the God essence in all , without fail. Anything that is happening to you, everything that you encounter, all that you see, hear and experience is a reflection of your belief. Whatever seems distasteful need only to be blessed away. Bless it. Praise it. Give thanks for every good and perfect thing regardless of its form and "be ye transformed, by the renewing of your mind."[36]

Negativity has no real power. It has only the power you give it by continued focus upon it. If you

---

[36] Romans 12:12

could take but a week where every thought, feeling, memory and projection were evaluated and those that contradicted the good were revised by faith, then the transformation of your affairs would begin so effortlessly, it would seem as if a miracle. There is a Light in all of us, a self-luminous beacon of perfect life, love and truth. In some, the inspiration of the divine is so untrammeled, that their light so flows fourth as to make their lives a benediction. These individuals allow the Light of Christ in them to shine without numerous obstructions. They are in communion with the flow of the Most-High. They feel, think and know the Source above all else. They live in gratitude, in joy, in kindness, in beauty and in love. They set forth an intention from deep within them of perfect faith in the Good.

Lift up thine self to reach the heights, the illumination glowing from the Most-High, the God within. Begin to give thanks religiously. Praise all, every time. Appreciate the small wonders, the modest gains. The Grace of God knows no size. Only the human mind differentiates and judges. The good that you see is your good! Embrace it. Accept it. Allow it to be the totality of who you are. Feel the abundance of grace. Give thanks from the core of your being, where Truth dwells. Be always in a state of thanksgiving. Appreciate the breath, the rich source behind each inhalation of pure substance. Relish in the moment to moment bounty available to you. Then release this gift, share and give, letting it go, only to be graced with another, purer than the last. This is the bounty of God.

Love

Your love is already here. The passion, adoration, intimacy and joy exists in all their fullness at this very moment. You do not have to wait any longer. The Master is here, loving you with more heart than you've ever dreamed. The heart of God envelopes you. You are loved and you love in return. The bond is mutual and unbreakable - a forever union. There is a perfect chemistry. You were made for one another. Nothing can come between you and your Love. The exchange is magical and it delights your soul. In this loving union, you are beautiful, so radiant, and your Lover reflects back to you your spectacular gaze. All is illumined in the light of your Love. There is nothing outside of your Love. All is One and the union is complete. Stop trying to make it happen out there. Find all within. Excavate the Truth from under the debris of false belief. That drama is not the other, but a reflection of your own inner turmoil. Forgive every last thing that you can think of which hurt you. Judge not another nor any action or experience. All is Good! You must know this if you want to be free. If you are ready to shed the weight, the time is now to know that nothing outside of you has any power but that which you give it!

Chapter 10

The I Am

I am waiting for you to realize, to see, that I alone am with you and my only goal is to love you. I am simple and pure. In order for me to love you, then you must look to me only and see your Truth. I am not an illusion, but the perfect Truth. I shine through all your cells, atoms and essence. I am the purity of your soul. Let me into your consciousness 100% of the time and I will transform your life. I am all the Good you dream of. Move aside and let me shine without shadow. I want to grace you, to bless you with my perfect love. I am made evident by praise.

Let gratitude be your only goal; your intention and your every impulse. You will never be more rich than you are now. You will never be more in love than you are right now. You will never be more whole than you are at this very moment. All the wealth that you will ever have, you possess right now. The totality of your prosperity is here, in all its greatness and magnitude. Your success is current and lives in the now. The greatest Love of your life is present with you today. There is nothing separating you from your perfect Good, but your own belief in its absence. There is never going to be a time more opportune than this very moment.

It is literally now or never. Your life is and always will be the sum of your beliefs about it right now. Your life is exactly what you imagine it to be. If you allow yourself only a small portion of Good in your beliefs, then only a small portion can come to you in your life experience. This is because it is actually coming through you and can only be as grand as you open yourself to greatness. You must inhabit the good you seek.

Prayer

I am all the wealth that I desire right now. I am so filled with my Love at this very moment that I am absolutely satisfied and content. I am truly whole in perfect health. I have it all now. I am prosperity and beyond today. I am in love with my perfect Love in wonderful union right now. I am perfectly whole. My home is the substance of God and I live freely here, now. My family is the heart of God which I now enjoy presently. My successful service to humanity is already done. All my Good is here. God is present with me, within me. I am complete. All is well with me. I am fully conscious now of my absolute perfection in this eternal moment and that there is nothing lacking in me or in my world. I am alive to face the perfect present where all is well.

I am now very wealthy, happy and whole. Right now, at this very moment, I have access to all the Good this universe has to offer. I have never been and will never be separated from the bountiful riches that are my Divine birthright, No matter what the appearances may say, In God, I Am the master of every earthly condition and can at will summon any good I desire. There can be no situation, circumstance or experience in my life which reflects anything but God's perfect Truth. This Truth is that I am rich with the Spirit, substance and form of God; that God is all that I am and therefore all abundance is mine to enjoy. I do not have to work for this abundance, nor sacrifice or struggle to obtain it. I have it naturally, by the Grace of God and cannot lose it by any means. It is not on its way to me. No, my absolute abundance is with me right now. It is who I am and what I am. I am not separate or apart from this Spirit, this substance, this form of God. I am that which it is

114

and am forever being so. I shall enact no rituals, perform no favors. I and my God are one and there is no good that is not already done in me. It would be my sin to fight and struggle against my true nature, my oneness with God, by allowing thoughts of worry, fear and lack to weigh down my perfect consciousness. I am the God in me which provides every good thing. There can absolutely be no lack or limitation. It is only in the mind where these falsities are conceived and imagined. They are not my reality and can never be. I shall turn from each thought contrary to God's perfect good now and embrace the boundless presence of that which I am. The good things of life are at hand and I shall claim them today. As I continuously praise the seemingly pervasive results of false thinking, these very challenges transform and my good blossoms as the rose. I smell roses all around me now. The scent of abundance fills every part of my being, its aroma saturating all space and I am become one with loveliness, peace and bounty. All my good is spilling forth now. It can hold itself no longer. Its angelic voice sings high into the heavens of my world and a chorus of perfection joins in. I am soaked with the magnetic waters of Christ's Spirit. Abundance dances forth from my interiors and colors the very essence of the air around me. I breathe in volumes of supply to fulfill every area of my life. I cannot halt the flow. It is everlasting and full. I bathe in the blessed substance of God and each cell of my being comes alive now with the power, presence and perfection of God. There is no tomorrow, nor yesterday. There is a place, a state of being free from all limitations, problems or discord, a place of true harmony and perfect peace. This place is now. And I Am here.

"I am closer to you than breathing, nearer than hands and feet."

~Alfred Tennyson

References

Ballard, Guy W. and St. Jermaine. (1999). *The I AM Discourses, Vols 1-3*. Schaumburg, IL: Saint Germaine Press.

Benner, Joseph. (2008). *The Way Out*. Camarillo, CA: Devorss and Company.

Goldsmith, Joel. (1977). *Showing Forth the Presence of God*. Atlanta, GA: Acropolis Books.

Hopkins, Emma Curtis. (1974). *Scientific Christian Mental Practice*. Camarillo, CA: Devorss & Company

Lanyon, Walter C. (1977). *The Temple Not Made With Hands*. Glen Ellyn, IL: Union Life Ministries.

Ponder, Catherine. (1990). *The Healing Secrets of the Ages*. Camarillo, CA: Devorss and Company

Spaulding, Baird T. (1986). *The Life and Teachings of the Masters of the Far East, Vol 1-7*. Camarillo, CA: Devorss & Company

The Holy Bible, King James Version . New York: American Bible Society: 1999; Bartleby.com, 2000.

Tolle, Eckhart. (1999).*The Power of Now: A Guide to Spiritual Enlightenment*. Novato, CA: New World Library.

Tolle, Eckhart. (2005). *A New Earth: Awakening to Your Life's Purpose*. New York: Penguin Group.

About the Author

Sia Alexander-Brume attended Stanford University and Howard University, graduating Magna Cum Laude with a BA in Human Psychology. Today Sia writes a blog which chronicles her journey of healing and service as she travels around the world

~ heallovenow.blogspot.com

Made in the USA
Middletown, DE
27 January 2023

23328936R00073